Atkinson

AF086336

by Iain Gray

WRITING *to* REMEMBER

WRITING *to* REMEMBER

79 Main Street, Newtongrange,
Midlothian EH22 4NA
Tel: 0131 344 0414   Fax: 0845 075 6085
E-mail: info@lang-syne.co.uk
www.langsyneshop.co.uk

Design by Dorothy Meikle
Printed by Printwell Ltd
© Lang Syne Publishers Ltd 2021

All rights reserved. No part of this publication may be reproduced, stored or introduced into a retrieval system, or transmitted in any form or by any means (electronic, mechanical, photocopying, recording or otherwise) without the prior written permission of Lang Syne Publishers Ltd.

ISBN 978-1-85217-802-4

Atkinson

MOTTO:
Hope in God

CREST:
An eagle

TERRITORY:
Cumbria and Northumberland

NAME variations include:
Acheson
Aitchison
Atkenson
Atkins
Attkinson
Aitkins
Aitkinson

Chapter one:

The origins of popular surnames

by George Forbes and Iain Gray

***If you don't know where you came from, you won't know where you're going** is a frequently quoted observation and one that has a particular resonance today when there has been a marked upsurge in interest in genealogy, with increasing numbers of people curious to trace their family roots.*

Main sources for genealogical research include census returns and official records of births, marriages and deaths – and the key to unlocking the detail they contain is obviously a family surname, one that has been 'inherited' and passed from generation to generation.

No matter our station in life, we all have a surname – but it was not until about the middle of the fourteenth century that the practice of being identified by a particular surname became commonly established throughout the British Isles.

Previous to this, it was normal for a person to be identified through the use of only a forename.

But as population gradually increased and there were many more people with the same forename, surnames were adopted to distinguish one person, or community, from another.

Many common English surnames are patronymic in origin, meaning they stem from the forename of one's father – with 'Johnson,' for example, indicating 'son of John.'

It was the Normans, in the wake of their eleventh century conquest of Anglo-Saxon England, a pivotal moment in the nation's history, who first brought surnames into usage – although it was a gradual process.

For the Normans, these were names initially based on the title of their estates, local villages and chateaux in France to distinguish and identify these landholdings.

Such grand descriptions also helped enhance the prestige of these warlords and generally glorify their lofty positions high above the humble serfs slaving away below in the pecking order who had only single names, often with Biblical connotations as in Pierre and Jacques.

The only descriptive distinctions among the peasantry concerned their occupations, like 'Pierre the swineherd' or 'Jacques the ferryman.'

Roots of surnames that came into usage in England not only included Norman-French, but also Old French, Old Norse, Old English, Middle English, German, Latin, Greek, Hebrew and the Gaelic languages of the Celts.

The Normans themselves were originally Vikings, or 'Northmen', who raided, colonised and eventually settled down around the French coastline.

They had sailed up the Seine in their longboats in 900AD under their ferocious leader Rollo and ruled the roost in north eastern France before sailing over to conquer England in 1066 under Duke William of Normandy – better known to posterity as William the Conqueror, or King William I of England.

Granted lands in the newly-conquered England, some of their descendants later acquired territories in Wales, Scotland and Ireland – taking not only their own surnames, but also the practice of adopting a surname, with them.

But it was in England where Norman rule and custom first impacted, particularly in relation to the adoption of surnames.

This is reflected in the famous *Domesday Book*, a massive survey of much of England and Wales, ordered by William I, to determine who owned what, what it was worth and therefore how much they were liable to pay in taxes to the voracious Royal Exchequer.

Completed in 1086 and now held in the National Archives in Kew, London, 'Domesday' was an Old English word meaning 'Day of Judgement.'

This was because, in the words of one contemporary chronicler, "its decisions, like those of the Last Judgement, are unalterable."

It had been a requirement of all those English landholders – from the richest to the poorest – that they identify themselves for the purposes of the survey and for future reference by means of a surname.

This is why the *Domesday Book*, although written in Latin as was the practice for several centuries with both civic and ecclesiastical records, is an invaluable source for the early appearance of a wide range of English surnames.

Several of these names were coined in connection with occupations.

These include Baker and Smith, while Cooks, Chamberlains, Constables and Porters were to be found carrying out duties in large medieval households.

The church's influence can be found in names such as Bishop, Friar and Monk while the popular name of Bennett derives from the late fifth to mid-sixth century Saint Benedict, founder of the Benedictine order of monks.

The early medical profession is represented by Barber, while businessmen produced names that include Merchant and Sellers.

Down at the village watermill, the names that cropped up included Millar/Miller, Walker and Fuller, while other self-explanatory trades included Cooper, Tailor, Mason and Wright.

Even the scenery was utilised as in Moor, Hill, Wood and Forrest – while the hunt and the chase supplied names that include Hunter, Falconer, Fowler and Fox.

Colours are also a source of popular surnames, as in Black, Brown, Gray/Grey, Green and White, and would have denoted the colour of the clothing the person habitually wore or, apart from the obvious exception of 'Green', one's hair colouring or even complexion.

The surname Red developed into Reid, while

Blue was rare and no-one wanted to be associated with yellow.

Rather self-important individuals took surnames that include Goodman and Wiseman, while physical attributes crept into surnames such as Small and Little.

Many families proudly boast the heraldic device known as a Coat of Arms, as featured on our front cover.

The central motif of the Coat of Arms would originally have been what was borne on the shield of a warrior to distinguish himself from others on the battlefield.

Not featured on the Coat of Arms, but highlighted on page three, is the family motto and related crest – with the latter frequently different from the central motif.

Adding further variety to the rich cultural heritage that is represented by surnames is the appearance in recent times in lists of the 100 most common names found in England of ones that include Khan, Patel and Singh – names that have proud roots in the vast sub-continent of India.

Echoes of a far distant past can still be found in our surnames and they can be borne with pride in commemoration of our forebears.

Chapter two:

Faith and resilience

Stemming from the Middle English personal name 'Atkin', in turn a pet form of the Biblically-derived 'Adam', 'Atkinson' denotes 'son of Atkin'.

Pre-dating the Norman Conquest of 1066, those who would come to bear it were to be found mainly in the north of England in the present-day local authority areas of Cumbria and Northumberland, while it is found over the nearby border with Scotland in forms that include 'Acheson' and 'Aitchison'.

Travelling back in time to late seventeenth and early eighteenth century England, Paul Atkinson, who was born Matthew Atkinson in about 1655 in Yorkshire, was the Roman Catholic priest who fell victim to harsh penal laws against the practise of his faith.

In 1558, about 100 years before his birth, The Act of Supremacy was passed under Queen Elizabeth I that confirmed her as Supreme Governor of the (Protestant) Church of England and also imposed an Oath of Supremacy requiring those holding church or public office to swear allegiance to her.

These measures were backed up by laws that ordered all Catholics who refused to swear to leave the country within 40 days – on pain of a charge of high treason, while similar punishment faced anyone harbouring priests.

Penalties ranged from fines and imprisonment to the ultimate sanction of being hanged, drawn and quartered, while it was not until as late as 1766 that these laws started to be gradually removed from the Statute Book.

Atkinson was among those loyal adherents of the faith who fled England and found refuge at Douai Abbey, also known as the English College – a Catholic seminary founded in France in 1561 by the Englishman William Allen.

A rallying point for exiled English Catholics, the abbey not only provided a safe haven for study and prayer but also acted as a training ground for what were known as 'seminary priests' who embarked on clandestine missions to their native shores to attempt the 're-conversion' from Protestantism to Catholicism.

Atkinson is thought to have arrived back in England in about 1688 and, with the covert aid of sympathisers who practised their faith in secret he managed to evade the authorities until betrayed by a maidservant in 1700.

Convicted and condemned to 'perpetual imprisonment' on September 26 of that year, he was confined in Hurst Castle, on the River Solent, for nearly 30 years until his death in 1729.

Considered a martyr because he spent his final days in prison due to his beliefs, he was later interred in the Roman Catholic cemetcry in Winchester.

While Paul Atkinson distinguished himself by selfless devotion, one particularly unsavoury bearer of the name by all accounts was the politician and merchant Christopher Atkinson, also known as Christopher Savile.

Born in the Catholic martyr's heartland of Yorkshire in 1738, he moved to London and married the daughter of a corn merchant and established himself in the business.

When wealth was then a means of entry into politics, he was elected MP (Member of Parliament) for the Yorkshire constituency of Hendon – but was expelled from the House of Commons three years later after being convicted of perjury.

His punishment included the public humiliation of being forced to stand in the pillory –

a wooden framework erected on a post with holes which secured his head and hands.

Atkinson obtained a royal pardon in 1791 and five years later returned to Parliament as MP for Hendon.

Buying a number of properties in Okehampton, Devon, he then represented that seat in Parliament from 1818 until a year before his death in 1820.

It was meanwhile after his second marriage to Jane Savile that he adopted the Savile surname, while his first marriage had been to Jane Constable, an aunt of the celebrated English painter John Constable.

Writing of his family history, the artist penned a rather less than flattering word portrait of Atkinson.

Describing him as "a man whose sole object in the world was gain" and that he would sacrifice every principle, he further condemned him with the observation he was "so hardened that reproach and shame would have no effect upon him."

Among the first group of convicts to be transported to New South Wales, George Atkinson, whose surname is also recorded as 'Atkins', was born in London in 1764.

A chimney sweep, he was aged 19 when caught in the act leaving a boarding house in the city's

Shoe Lane carrying a bundle containing a cloth coat, four pairs of breeches, four shirts, two waistcoats, a pair of shoes and stockings, two handkerchiefs and a book identified as belonging to one of the lodgers.

Put on trial and offering no defence, in keeping with the harsh punishment of the time for what today would be regarded as a fairly trivial offence of theft, he was sentenced to seven years of penal servitude.

This would normally have been served in the British colonies in the Americas but that was no longer possible because of the American Revolutionary War.

Instead, he spent three miserable years confined in the fetid depths of the prison hulk *Censor*, moored in the River Thames.

In February of 1787, he was taken along with fellow prisoners to Portsmouth to the convict ship *Scarborough* and transported as part of what is known to posterity as the First Fleet to the Australian penal colony of New South Wales.

Arriving in Port Jackson in January of the following year, he remained there until transferred as a labourer on a government farm on Norfolk Island.

His sentence expired in 1791 and, in common with many other former convicts, George chose to remain and embarked on a number of careers including farming, as a seaman and – rather ironically – in law enforcement.

Later purchasing a sea-going sloop and having married fellow convict Mary Cockran in 1792, he became one of the colony's earliest ship owners.

But the enterprise failed and he returned to working variously as a police constable and night watchman before his death in Sydney in 1834.

One particularly adventurous and resilient bearer of the Atkinson name was Lucy Sherrard Atkinson, the English explorer, traveller and author born Lucy Sherrard Finley in Sunderland, County Durham, in 1817.

The fourth of ten children of schoolmaster Matthew Finley and Mary Ann York, daughter of a perfumer, it was while living in St Petersburg as governess to the family of a high-ranking member of the Russian nobility that she met the English explorer and former architect Thomas Witlam Atkinson, nearly twenty years her senior.

The couple married in St Petersburg in 1848 and immediately embarked on a hazardous trek throughout Siberia, south to the Kazakh steppes and then eastwards to as far as the border with China – a journey of more than 4,000 miles.

Adding to the rigours of the trek was that in its early stages Lucy had been pregnant with their son who, born on the Kazakh Steppe, was named Alatau Tamchiboulac Atkinson – his first name from the Alatau Mountains and the second from a spring famous for its healing powers.

The family returned to Britain in 1858 and, settling in London, Thomas Atkinson penned two books on his travels. Oddly, however, neither book mentions his wife or son – the reason being that he wished to deflect attention away from them because he had, in fact, married Lucy bigamously. His first wife, from whom he had separated before leaving for Russia, was still alive and living in London.

The couple continued to live together, however, and it was two years after her husband's death in 1861 that Lucy published her celebrated *Recollections of Tartar Steppes and Their Inhabitants* – one of the first travel books of its kind to be written in English by a woman.

She died in 1893 while her son Alatau, after working for a time as a journalist and schoolteacher in Newcastle, immigrated to Hawaii.

Becoming a newspaper owner and serving as inspector general of schools, he died in 1906.

Chapter three:

Science and invention

An impressive number of advances in the sciences and other areas of human endeavour have been made by bearers of the Atkinson name.

In the constantly evolving world of information technology, Bill Atkinson is the American engineer responsible for the creation of a range of software tools.

Born in 1959 and employed by Apple Inc. from 1978 to 1990, he was the inventor of the MacPaint application and designer of the QuickDraw toolbox.

One of the first thirty members of founder Steve Jobs' original Apple Macintosh team, he also conceived and designed the hypermedia system HyperCard, and in 1994 was the recipient of the EEF (Electronic Frontier Foundation) Pioneer Award.

Portrayed by the actor Nelson Franklin in the 2013 biopic *Jobs*, he now concentrates his creative talents on nature photography.

A leading British scientist of the twentieth century, James Atkinson was the radar pioneer whose work made a significant contribution towards Allied victory in the Second World War.

Born in 1916 in Wallington, London, after graduating from St John's College, Cambridge a year before the outbreak of the war, he was employed as a researcher at the Air Ministry Research Establishment in Bawsdey Manor, Suffolk.

It was here that he carried out work on cathode ray tubes and, later, on the series of Chain Home radar stations set up at strategic locations throughout the country to detect and give early warning of approaching enemy aircraft.

Also engaged in research into special infra-red detectors for guided missile weapons, after the war he was a member of the University of Glasgow's department of natural philosophy, where he undertook work on the 'photo-disintegration' of nuclei by bombardment with gamma rays.

Leaving the university in 1958 to take up the post of deputy director of research at the Dounreay nuclear establishment in Scotland and later holding other positions including deputy director of the Institute of Offshore Engineering at Heriot-Watt University, Edinburgh, he died in 1964.

In the highly cerebral realms of mathematics,

Frederick Valentine Atkinson, more familiarly known as Derick Atkinson, was the noted British mathematician born in 1916 in Pinner, Middlesex.

A graduate of The Queen's College, Oxford, in common with James Atkinson he also carried out vital work during the Second World War – in his case at the top secret Government Code and Cypher School at Bletchley Park, Buckinghamshire.

This was where German military intercepts were decoded with the aid of the 'Enigma' device, giving the Allies invaluable warning of enemy strategy, logistics and future plans.

A number of academic appointments followed after the war including, from 1960 until his retirement in 1982, professor of mathematics at the University of Toronto.

The recipient of a number of honours and awards including fellowship of the Royal Society of Canada and winner of the 1992 Alexander Von Humboldt Research Award, he died in 2002 while the mathematical Atkinson's theorem and the Atkinson-Wilcox theorem are named after him.

Bearers of the Atkinson name have also been pioneers in the academic discipline of economics, with Sir Anthony Barnes Atkinson, more popularly known as Tony Atkinson, recognised today as having been 'virtually single-handedly' responsible for the establishment of the British field of poverty and inequality studies.

Born in 1944 in Caerleon, Wales, he switched from studying mathematics at the University of Oxford to economics, graduating with a first class degree in 1966.

Previous to this, he had worked for a time at IBM after leaving school when aged 17 and then spending a year in Germany working as a volunteer in a hospital in a deprived area of Hamburg.

It was this experience that appears to have stirred his interest in the links between inequality and poverty and, after further in-depth studies at institutions including the Massachusetts Institute of Technology (MIT), he developed his theories.

Teaching public economics at St John's College, Cambridge from 1967 to 1971, his lectures were collated into what has become the famous textbook *Lectures in Public Economics* while, later holding other academic posts, he also founded the *Journal of Public Economics*.

Working in areas ranging from wealth distribution and taxation to the economics of poverty, the welfare state and health, he examined how public policy is disproportionately influenced by the wealthy.

Developing the measure of inequality the Atkinson index, he was also an advocate for the introduction of a basic income.

The recipient of honours and awards including fellowship of the Econometric Society, Honorary Member of the American Economic Association and a knighthood, he died in 2017.

An American pioneer in the field of enhancing the quality of life of the visually impaired, J. Robert Atkinson was born in 1887 in Galt, Missouri.

Blinded in a gun accident when aged 16 while working as a cowboy in Montana, he overcame severe depression because of his condition by learning the reading tool for the blind known as Braille, and also teaching others.

With the financial backing of the philanthropist Mary Beecher Longyear, in 1919 he founded the Universal Braille Printing Press – now the Braille Institute of America – which in 1924 published the first Braille edition of the King James Version of the Bible.

Also the founder in 1926 of *Braille Mirror* magazine, a digest of contemporary articles covering a range of subjects, he died in 1964, while in 2002 he was posthumously inducted into the Hall of Fame: Leaders and Legends of the Blindness Field.

A bearer of the Atkinson name who truly found himself at the centre of international events in the 1970s was the British aviator Neville Atkinson, born in 1933 in Beverley, East Riding of Yorkshire.

Having served in the Fleet Air Arm of the Royal Navy, piloting Sea Vixen FAW2 fighters from HMS *Centaur*, he left the service in 1972 to take up the position of personal pilot to Libyan president Colonel Gaddafi.

It was as Gaddafi's pilot that in December of 1975 he was given the task of flying Ilich Ramirez Sánchez, better known as the infamous Venezuelan-born terrorist Carlos the Jackal, following an attack on the Vienna headquarters of OPEC (Organisation of the Petroleum Exporting Countries).

A supporter of the PLO (Popular Front for the Liberation of Palestine) and having already carried out a number of highly-publicised attacks on Western targets on its behalf, on December 21, 1975 the Jackal and a six-man team stormed a meeting of OPEC leaders.

Taking more than 60 hostages, they killed three of them including an Austrian policeman.

Tense negotiations for the release of the others followed, with the Jackal demanding the Austrian authorities read out a communique about the Palestinian cause on radio and television every two hours.

Threatening the execution of a hostage every fifteen minutes unless his demands were met, the authorities complied and, the following day, further agreed to provide an aircraft to fly the Jackal and his team and the remaining hostages to Algiers.

Following further negotiations, it was agreed the pilot would be the hapless Neville Atkinson – whose employer Gaddafi was known for his support of a number of terrorist organisations.

Provided with a DC-9 aircraft, he flew from Vienna to Algiers, where a number of hostages were released, then to the Libyan capital Tripoli for the release of more and, finally, back to Algiers where the remainder and the Jackal and his team were allowed to disembark.

One moment of light relief in an otherwise highly dangerous situation is reputed to have come when Atkinson asked the Jackal to sign a copy of the best-selling Frederick Forsyth novel *The Day of the Jackal*.

It had been following publication of the book in 1971 that Ilich Ramirez Sánchez was first dubbed 'The Jackal' after a journalist apparently spotted a copy among some of his abandoned possessions.

Eventually captured and brought to justice by a French court in 1997, Carlos the Jackal was found guilty of the murder of two policemen in Paris in 1975 and sentenced to life imprisonment without the possibility of parole.

Atkinson, who continued to serve as Gaddafi's personal pilot until 1982, died one year after the publication in 2006 of his auto-biographical *Death on Small Wings: Memoirs of a Presidential Pilot*.

Chapter four:

On the world stage

Born in 1955 in Consett, County Durham, Rowan Atkinson is the English comedian, actor and writer originally destined for a career in the much different worlds of science and engineering.

The recipient of a degree in electrical and electronic engineering from the University of Newcastle and an MSc (Master of Science) from Queen's College, Oxford, it was while at the latter institution that he first took to the stage through its dramatic society.

Performing in the Oxford Revue at the Edinburgh Festival Fringe in 1975, from 1979 to 1982 he came to prominence on the television screen through the BBC sketch show *Not the Nine O'Clock News*.

Gaining further acclaim on the small screen with the sitcoms *Blackadder* and, from 1990 to 1995, *Mr Bean*, film credits include the 1983 James Bond *Never Say Never Again*, the 1994 *Four Weddings and a Funeral* and, from 2003, *Love Actually* – while from 2003 to 2018 he starred in the *Johnny English* comedy series.

A frequent collaborator on television and film productions with the screenwriter Richard Curtis and composer Howard Goodall – both of whom he first met while at Oxford – he was appointed a CBE in 2013 for services to drama and charity.

From the stage to politics, his older brother **Rodney Atkinson**, born in 1948, is the political and economic commentator, academic and author who in 2000 stood unsuccessfully for the leadership of the UK Independence Party (UKIP).

Returning to the stage, **Ashlie Atkinson**, born in 1977 in Little Rock, Arkansas, is the American character actress whose television credits include *Happy!* and *Mr Robot*.

The recipient of a 2004 Theatre World Award for Outstanding Off-Broadway Debut for her role of plus-size librarian Helen in the play *Fat Pig*, her big screen credits include the 2019 *Juanita*.

Back on British shores, **Gemma Atkinson**, born in 1984 in Bury, Greater Manchester is the actress and former fashion model whose television credits include the soaps *Hollyoaks*, *Casualty* and *Emmerdale*.

Born in 1966 in Mansfield, Nottinghamshire, **Dorothy Atkinson** is the actress and singer who, in addition to appearing in a number of plays by Alan Ayckbourn, has also starred in films by Mike Leigh including the 2014 *Mr Turner*.

Known for her role of Karen Maguire from 2004 to 2013 in the television comedy drama series *Shameless*, **Rebecca Atkinson** is the English actress born in 1983 in Salford, Manchester.

With other television credits including *Life on Mars*, *Holby City*, *Coronation Street* and *River City*, she also appears in the 2009 film *Awaydays*.

Named by the *New York Times* as "the theatre's most influential reviewer of his time", **Justin Atkinson** was the newspaper's celebrated critic from 1922 until his retirement in 1960.

Born in 1894 in Melrose, Massachusetts, his reviews were said to have had the power to make or break a new production, while he was one of the first admirers of the great American playwright Eugene O'Neill.

Serving throughout the Second World War as a correspondent on the battlefield for the *New York Times*, he was awarded the Pulitzer Prize two years after the end of the conflict for his work as the newspaper's Moscow representative.

Elected a Fellow of the American Academy of Arts and Sciences, he died in 1984.

Bearers of the Atkinson name have also excelled in the highly competitive world of sport.

On the fields of European football Ronald Atkinson, better known as **Ron Atkinson** or 'Big Ron', is the English former player and manager born in Liverpool in 1939 but moving shortly after his birth to Warwickshire.

Spending most of his career at Oxford United and making more than 500 appearances as a wing-half throughout the 1960s, teams he managed include Aston Villa, Sheffield United, West Bromwich Albion and Manchester United – winning the FA Cup with the latter in both 1983 and 1985.

A popular pundit on the game throughout the 1990s and 2000s, he is the older brother of **Graham Atkinson**, born in 1943 and who died in 2017 and who played beside him for a time at Oxford United.

On the cricket pitch **Denis Atkinson** was the West Indian player born in 1926 in Rockley, Christ Church, who still holds the record for bowling the highest number of wicketless overs in a Test innings.

This was when in 1957 he recorded 72 overs, 29 maidens, no wicket for 137 runs for the West

Indies against England at Edgbaston, Birmingham; he died in 2001, while his younger brother **Eric Atkinson**, born in 1927 and who died in 1998, was also a noted West Indies player.

In the world of extreme sport and truly scaling record heights, **George Atkinson**, born in 1994 in Surrey, is the English climber who, when aged 16, became the youngest person ever to complete the Seven Summits Challenge by reaching the top of the highest mountain on all of the seven continents.

Beginning the challenge when aged only 11, he accomplished it over a six-year period and just a few days short of his seventeenth birthday.

First on the gruelling list was Mount Kilimanjaro, Africa's highest mountain followed, when aged 13, by Mount Elbrus, in Europe.

Just before his fourteenth birthday he successfully tackled Australasia's Puncak Jaya, followed in succession over the years by Aconcagua in South America, Mount Denali in North America and Antarctica's Mount Vinson.

His crowning glory came on May 26, 2011, when he reached the summit of Mount Everest on the Asian continent.

Aged 16 years and 362 days, he beat the previous record of 17 years and 296 days old by American Johnny Collinson – only to be surpassed just over seven months later by 15-year-old American Justin Romero.

In the creative world of literature, **Kate Atkinson** is the award-winning English novelist, playwright and short story writer born in 1951 in York – the setting for many of her books.

Gaining a master's degree in English literature in 1974 after studying at the University of Dundee, she is best known for her Jackson Brodie series of detective novels that have been adapted for television as *Case Histories*.

Winner of the 1995 Whitbread Book of the Year Award in the novels category for *Behind the Scenes at the Museum*, her other awards include the 2013 Costa Award for *Life after Life* and, in 2015, *A God in Ruins*.

Also the author of the 2019 *Sky*, she was appointed an MBE in 2011 for services to literature.

Across the Atlantic, Lawrence Rush Atkinson IV is the American author better known as **Rick Atkinson**.

Born in Munich, Germany, in 1952 where his

father was serving with the U.S. Army, and the winner of Pulitzer prizes in history and journalism, as a military historian he is best known for his Liberation Trilogy, chronicling America's role in Allied victory in Europe during the Second World War and which includes the 2013 *The Guns at Last Light*.

From the written word to the equally creative world of music, **Paul Atkinson** was the British guitarist and record company executive born in 1946 in Cuffley, Hertfordshire.

A founding member of the pop/rock band the Zombies, whose hits include the 1964 *She's Not There*, as an A&R (Artists and Repertoire) executive for Dick James Music, he was instrumental in the signing of bands and artists including ABBA, Elton John and Judas Priest.

He died in 2004 and was posthumously inducted five years later into the Rock and Roll Hall of Fame.

One bearer of the Atkinson name with a rather unusual claim to fame is **James Henry Atkinson**, the ironmonger from Leeds, in England, who in 1899 patented a mousetrap still sold throughout the world to this day.

Although the basic style of the spring-loaded

mousetrap was patented five years earlier by the American inventor William Chauncey Hooker, Atkinson's simple device, known as the Little Nipper, and consisting of a spring-loaded hinged metal bar mounted on a small, flat wooden base, has proven the most popular.

Atkinson, who died in 1942, sold his patent to the American company Procter – now Procter and Gamble – in 1913 for £1000, the equivalent of nearly £66,000 today.